RICHARD NIXON

ENCYCLOPEDIA
of PRESIDENTS

Richard Nixon

Thirty-Seventh President of the United States

By Dee Lillegard

Consultant: Charles Abele, Ph.D.
Social Studies Instructor
Chicago Public School System

CHILDRENS PRESS ®

CHICAGO

President Eisenhower and Vice-President Nixon at the 1956 Republican national convention

Library of Congress Cataloging-in-Publication Data

Lillegard, Dee.
  Richard Nixon / by Dee Lillegard.
        p.   cm. — (Encyclopedia of presidents)
  Includes index.
  Summary: Follows the life and career of the first American
president to resign from office.
  ISBN 0-516-01356-4
  1. Nixon, Richard M. (Richard Milhous), 1913-   —
Juvenile literature.   2.   Presidents—United States—
Biography—Juvenile literature.   [1.   Nixon, Richard M.
(Richard Milhous), 1913-   2.   Presidents.]
I. Title. II. Series.
E856.L55   1988
973.924'092'4—dc19   87-35185
[B]   CIP
[92]   AC

Picture Acknowledgments

AP/Wide World Photos—4, 5, 6, 11, 14, 23, 25,
28, 35, 39, 50, 55, 62, 66 (2 photos), 67 (top),
70, 71, 73 (2 photos), 79, 81, 82, 86, 89

Historical Pictures Service, Chicago—34, 36, 43

UPI/Bettmann Newsphotos—9, 12, 13, 17, 18,
19, 21, 24, 26, 27, 32, 40, 44, 45, 46, 47, 49, 53,
54, 57 (2 photos), 58, 59, 61, 67 (bottom), 68,
69, 76, 83, 85, 88

U.S. Bureau of Printing and Engraving—2

Cover design and illustration by
Steven Gaston Dobson

Childrens Press®, Chicago
Copyright ©1988 by Regensteiner Publishing Enterprises, Inc.
All rights reserved. Published simultaneously in Canada.
Printed in the United States of America.
  2 3 4 5 6 7 8 9 10 R 97 96 95 94 93 92 91 90 89

Nixon and his family during the 1952 campaign: left to right are his mother, Hannah; Richard; daughter Patricia; wife, Pat; daughter Julie; and father, Frank.

Table of Contents

Chapter 1

A Dog Named Checkers

In 1951, at the age of thirty-eight, Richard Nixon was the youngest member of the United States Senate—and one of the busiest. His secretary, Rose Mary Woods, had to "run along beside him," taking notes as he headed for the Senate floor. "In a few minutes," Woods said, "he can give me a list of twenty phone calls to make [and] twice as many notes to write. . . ."

Nixon had been in politics only four years before becoming a Republican senator from California, the second largest state. He was already well known across the nation. There were even rumors that he might be considered for the Republican vice-presidential nomination in the election of 1952.

Richard Nixon and his wife, Pat, hardly had time to think about the rumors. Nixon was busy serving in the Senate and making speeches around the country to help other Republicans raise funds. Democrats had controlled the nation politically since 1933, and Nixon knew that Republican candidates running for Congress needed all the help they could get. He also knew that the Republicans would have to have a strong candidate for president if they were going to win in 1952. Several worthy contenders were being considered for the Republican presidential nomination, but Nixon believed only one of them could win—General Dwight David Eisenhower.

Ike, as Eisenhower was popularly known, was a World War II hero. In 1951, he was serving as the Supreme Commander of the American and European troops that were part of the North Atlantic Treaty Organization (NATO). The Draft Eisenhower for President League in Washington was already chanting "I Like Ike" when Nixon was sent to Europe that spring. He was a Senate observer to the World Health Organization conference in Geneva, Switzerland.

On a side trip to Paris, France, where Eisenhower was headquartered, Senator Nixon met with the general. Ike said he had heard good things about Nixon. He liked Nixon's speeches and his ideas. Nixon, in turn, was awed by this world-famous military hero.

Another strong Eisenhower supporter was Thomas Dewey, governor of New York. Dewey had run for president against Harry Truman in 1948 and lost. On May 8, 1952, at Dewey's request, Nixon gave the main speech at a New York Republican fund-raising dinner. Dewey thought Nixon gave "a terrific speech." Afterwards, he mentioned the possibility of Nixon's being a vice-presidential candidate. Surprised, Nixon said he would consider it.

Two months later, on July 11, 1952, the Republicans held their national convention in Chicago, Illinois. They nominated Eisenhower to be their presidential candidate. At the end of a long day, Nixon returned to his hotel room, exhausted, and lay down to rest. "I had just started to drift off to sleep," he later wrote, "when the bedside phone rang." The message was that Eisenhower had chosen Nixon to be his running mate, if Nixon would accept. Could he come and see the general right away?

Rose Mary Woods, Nixon's personal secretary, helps him sort his mail.

In rumpled clothes, badly needing a shower and a shave, Senator Nixon dashed off to meet with General and Mrs. Eisenhower. Then he hurried to the convention hall, where he would be nominated that evening.

Pat was having a sandwich in a restaurant when a flash bulletin on the restaurant television announced Nixon's candidacy. Later she told reporters she was "amazed, flabbergasted, weak, and speechless." She rushed off to join her husband, leaving her sandwich unfinished.

The Nixons did not know it then, but they were in for a less pleasant surprise. On September 18, 1952, after an exciting homecoming in southern California, Nixon began his campaign. Like the other candidates, he started a "whistle-stop" tour of the country in a special train. Nixon's train had barely begun to roll when a New York newspaper headline blared: SECRET NIXON FUND!

The newspaper said Nixon was receiving thousands of dollars a year from a group of California businessmen—which was true. It also claimed that Nixon was using the money to live in high style—which was not true. The money was used to pay only political expenses.

Everywhere the train stopped, Nixon had to defend himself. He explained that there was nothing improper about such funds so long as they were not used for personal purposes. Many politicians received much-needed help in this way. Nevertheless, a lot of people felt that Eisenhower should drop Nixon from the ticket.

Eisenhower could not decide what to do, and neither could Nixon. Although innocent of any wrongdoing, he wondered if he should drop out of the campaign or fight for his honor, as Pat insisted.

Finally Ike called Nixon and said, "I think you ought to go on a nationwide television program and tell [the people] everything there is to tell."

Nixon's whole career as a politician was hanging by a thread. Television was something new. He had had no experience with it. What should he say? How should he say it? Then Nixon received an unexpected boost.

The newspapers reported that the Democratic presidential candidate, Adlai Stevenson, had a fund very much like Nixon's. Stevenson did not deny this. Encouraged, Nixon worked feverishly to prepare his speech. Then, minutes before he was to go on television, he received a call from Dewey. Dewey said Eisenhower's top advisers thought he should announce that he was dropping out. Dewey even suggested that Nixon resign his Senate seat.

Nixon naps on the plane on the way to make his "explanation" speech.

Nixon was badly shaken. With Pat's help, he pulled himself together to address the largest audience, till then, in the history of humanity. Fifty-eight million Americans watched as Richard Nixon spoke. He not only explained the fund, he told them everything about his and Pat's personal finances. He challenged Stevenson to do the same.

It was clear that the Nixons were not living in high style. It also seemed clear that Nixon had not accepted political gifts for his personal use. He then talked about a gift he and his family had taken for very personal reasons.

"You know what it was?" he said. "It was a little cocker spaniel dog . . . black and white spotted. And our little girl—Tricia, the six-year-old—named it Checkers. And you know the kids love that dog and . . . regardless of what they say about it, we're going to keep it."

Nixon and Eisenhower, the Republican team

Then Nixon asked the viewers to write in their decisions: Should he stay on the ticket or get off?

When his now-famous "Checkers speech" was over, Nixon apologized to his friends. "It was a flop," he said. But they insisted he had done a great job. When he returned to his hotel, there was a crowd to cheer him. Someone shouted, "The telephones are going crazy; everybody's in your corner!" In the next few days, more than a million people responded overwhelmingly in his favor.

In their hotel room in Cleveland, Ohio, Ike and Mamie Eisenhower had watched the speech. It brought tears to Mamie's eyes and helped Ike make up his mind. A few days later, the general—who was to be the next president of the United States—greeted Richard Nixon with the welcome words: "You're my boy."

Senator and Mrs. Nixon flash elated smiles as the cameras snap away.
Nixon has just received the 1952 vice-presidential nomination, and he and
Pat are on the rostrum during the acceptance speeches.

Chapter 2

A Small-Town Boy

Richard Nixon's family was neither rich nor famous, but they could point to a proud heritage in this country. On his father's side, the Nixons were boisterous, lively Methodists. On his mother's side, the Milhouses were gentle, quiet Quakers. Both families, however, were workers and builders who had moved west with the frontier.

The Nixons originally came from Scotland. They migrated to Ireland in the early 1600s and then, in the 1730s, to America. Nixons fought in the revolutionary war, and Richard's grandfather, George Nixon, died at the Battle of Gettysburg during the Civil War.

Richard's father, Frank Nixon, was born in Ohio. His family was poor, and life at home was not happy. Frank's mother died when he was seven, and his stepmother was a cruel woman who beat him. At age fourteen he left home.

Frank wandered from city to city, state to state, taking on different jobs. He painted railroad cars, sheared sheep, worked as a carpenter, and installed early hand-crank telephones. One harsh winter in Ohio, when he was working as a streetcar motorman, his feet were badly frostbitten. From then on they pained him in cold weather. So Frank Nixon moved to the warm climate of southern California, where he would meet Hannah Milhous.

Opposite page: Frank and Hannah Nixon
with Harold, Donald, and Richard

The Milhous family (originally Melhausen) migrated from Germany to England in 1688. There they became Quakers, or members of the Society of Friends. From England they moved to Ireland and then to America, where they could practice their faith freely. The Quakers were stern, hard-working people who were against war, alcoholic drinks, and even music and dancing. They strongly believed in justice for all human beings. Around the time of the Civil War, Milhouses helped runaway slaves escape through the "Underground Railroad."

Hannah Milhous, born in Indiana, grew up in the Quaker town of Whittier, fifteen miles from Los Angeles, California. Her peaceful Quaker family was not happy to see their soft-spoken Hannah being courted by Frank Nixon. He was a stormy fellow who liked to argue. For Frank, it was "love at first sight." He and Hannah married in June 1908, just four months after they met, and Frank became a Quaker.

The Nixons' first child, Harold, was born in 1909. Three years later, Frank bought a lemon ranch in Yorba Linda, a new town near Whittier. On January 9, 1913, Richard Milhous Nixon was born in a small white house that his father had built. It was a far cry from the White House he was destined to occupy.

There would be five sons in all for Frank and Hannah. Donald was born in 1914, Arthur in 1918, and Edward in 1930. Richard was named after Richard the Lion-Hearted, a king of England. He had such a "powerful ringing voice" as a baby that his Grandma Milhous said he would be "either a lawyer or a preacher" when he grew up.

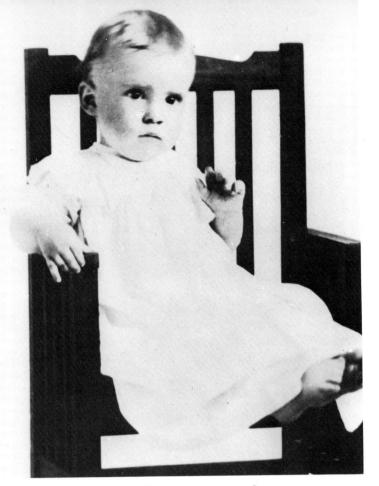

Richard Nixon at nine months

Richard Nixon very nearly did not grow up. When he was three years old, Hannah was driving him and baby Donald in a horse-drawn buggy. Richard would not sit down, and when the horse went around a corner, he fell out of the buggy. As the wagon wheel brushed past his head, it left a deep cut. He had to be rushed to the nearest doctor, twenty-five miles away, who stitched his scalp back together. The long scar it left would later govern the way Richard Nixon combed his hair.

During Richard's early years, the Nixon family lived on the edge of poverty. Later Hannah recalled, "Many days I had nothing to serve but corn meal!"

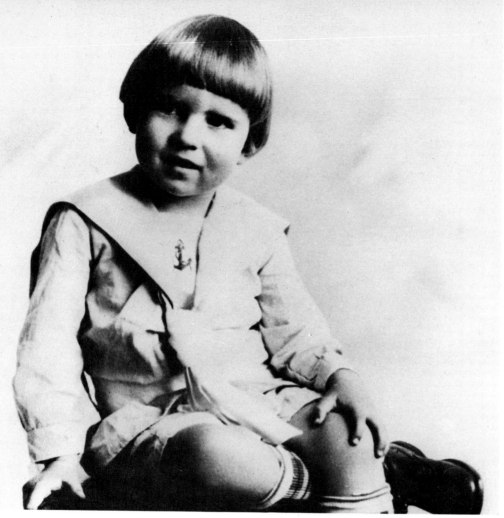

Five-year-old Richard in sailor suit, high-button shoes, and Buster Brown haircut

The lemon ranch was not profitable, and Frank had to support his family by doing odd jobs. A skilled carpenter, he built many of the homes that still stand in Yorba Linda. Frank was one of Richard's most important teachers. He taught Sunday school, which Richard attended regularly after the age of five. In his classes, Frank gave lively talks about politics and the need for practicing Christianity in public affairs. By the age of six, Richard was reading the newspapers—the news, not the comics—and discussing current events with his father.

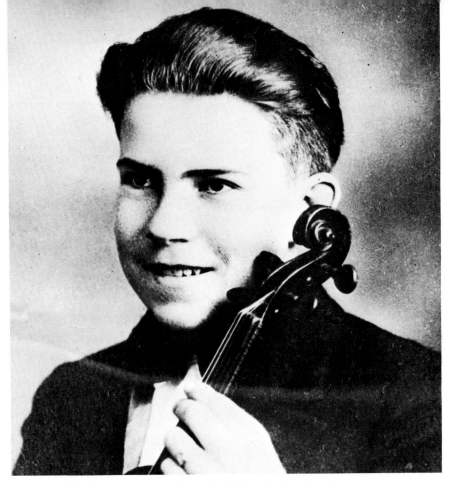

Richard as a violinist in his high school orchestra

Richard was a serious child, his mother recalled. "He was very mature even when he was five or six years old." He also spent time daydreaming, often lying on his back for hours gazing up at the sky. At night, in the small bedroom he shared with Harold and Arthur, he would listen to the distant train whistle and dream of traveling to faraway places. He wanted to be a railroad engineer.

Though Richard was shy, he always enjoyed reciting. He had an excellent memory and liked to speak before an audience. He also loved music and had a natural talent for it. At seven, Richard started piano and violin lessons. Later he became an accomplished pianist.

In 1922, when Richard was nine, Frank sold his house and moved the family back to Whittier. Though it was not far from Hollywood and the glamorous young movie industry, Whittier remained a quiet Quaker town, with many orange and avocado groves. The automobile had not yet come into its own, and few roads were paved. Even so, Frank could see the need for a gas station in just the right place. As the president later recalled, his father "borrowed $5,000 to buy some land on the main road connecting the growing towns of Whittier and La Habra. He cleared the lot, put in a tank and a pump, and opened the first service station in the eight-mile stretch between the two towns."

Frank's gamble turned out to be the right choice. From the start, business was good. Soon Frank added boxes of fruits and vegetables—and Hannah's pies—to the tires he was selling. When the Quakers built a new church, he bought the old one, had it moved to his lot, and opened it as a general store. Later he leased the gas station to a neighbor. The store alone provided plenty of work for the whole Nixon family.

Richard worked hard not only in the Nixon store but also to get top grades all through school. Frank had had to leave school after the sixth grade, and he often told his sons how lucky they were to be able to get an education. The president later remembered, "My biggest thrill in those years was to see the light in his eyes when I brought home a good report card. . . ."

Frank loved to argue about politics. Sometimes he upset his family and his customers by shouting. In school, Richard showed talent for a formal kind of argument

An undated photograph from Nixon's early years

called debate. He could take any side of a question and win a debate with facts and calm reasoning. He never shouted. By the eighth grade, he was already a champion debater.

In the summer of 1925, when Richard was twelve, his brother Arthur became ill. Arthur did not want to eat and began to sleep more and more.

Doctors took tests and shook their heads, unable to find a cause for his illness. In August, Arthur died. Richard sank into a deep silence. Years later he wrote, "For weeks after Arthur's funeral there was not a day that I did not think about him and cry."

The following year, in 1926, Richard entered high school in nearby Fullerton. His work load increased. With schoolwork, study, the store, and church, he hardly had time to sleep. Yet he went out for football, basketball, and track and showed up for practice every day. Many times this meant studying well past midnight.

Richard and his family had another tragedy to face. Harold developed tuberculosis, or TB, a disease of the lungs. At the time, people believed that a dry climate would help TB patients. So Frank and Hannah drove to Prescott, in the dry Arizona mountains, where Hannah rented a cabin. She insisted upon taking care of Harold herself and took in three other TB patients to pay the rent. This left Frank, Richard, and Don alone to run the store.

Richard spent the summers of 1928 and 1929 in Prescott, staying in the cabin where his mother cared for her four TB patients. He did little more than spend nights there because he was working every waking hour to help his family. Richard labored in the fields for twenty-five cents an hour, worked as a janitor, and plucked and dressed chickens for a butcher. He even held a job as a carnival barker or announcer. "Dick's Wheel of Fortune" made the most money of any of the carnival concessions.

In 1928, when school bus service began to Whittier High School, Richard (also called Dick) transferred there from Fullerton. In his junior year, he decided to study law and become a politician. Because he believed that successful politicians are joiners, he joined the Latin Club, the debate team, and the school newspaper. He played violin in the school orchestra and continued to participate in sports.

Richard Nixon
in his young
adulthood

In the spring of 1929, he won a Kiwanis Club speech contest on a favorite subject of his—the U.S. Constitution.

In his senior year, Richard won the Harvard Club of California's award for "best all-around student." With the award came a scholarship to Harvard, a fine but expensive university in the East. The scholarship would help, but it would not cover all expenses.

A month before Richard graduated from high school, Hannah gave birth to her fifth son, Edward. The new baby, along with Harold's illness, was costing the Nixons all they could earn. A worldwide economic crisis that had begun in 1929 had plunged the United States into the Great Depression. Money was hard to come by, and jobs were hard to get. As a result, Richard had to say no to Harvard. But this disappointment did not stop him from continuing his education.

Richard (number 12) in his senior year at Whittier College

In the fall of 1930, Richard entered Whittier College, which his mother had attended years before. He participated in more than fifty debates and won most of them. His football career was less successful, although he worked hard to make the team. A teammate recalled, "He was little, but he had more fight and spunk than the big men." Even though he was not skilled at the game, he constantly cheered the team on and was quick to give pep talks to injured players.

Nixon's senior portrait, Whittier College, class of 1934

Richard loved the stage and participated in every play at Whittier during his college years. He also sang in the College Glee Club. All this time he was getting up at four o'clock every morning and driving to Los Angeles to buy produce at the farmers' market for the family store. He then had to drive back home and set up the fruits and vegetables before school. On top of that, on afternoons and weekends he did the bookkeeping for the store.

Nixon's college graduation picture

In the meantime, Harold was wasting away. Richard loved and admired his older brother. Harold's death in March 1933 was another terrible blow to him. Though grieving the loss of his brother, Richard continued to work as hard as ever. That fall, in his last year at Whittier, he was elected president of the student body. He graduated from Whittier in June 1934, ranking second in his class.

After graduation, young Nixon applied for a scholarship to Duke University Law School in North Carolina. The

Duke University Law School, class of 1937. Richard Nixon is in the top row on the right.

president of Whittier College wrote in a letter to Duke: "I
cannot recommend him too highly because I believe that
Nixon will become one of America's important, if not
great leaders." Duke awarded the future president of the
United States a scholarship.

Whittier College could have fit into one small corner of
the impressive Duke campus, three thousand miles from
Whittier. Nixon's years at Duke would take him a long
way from the small-town life he had known.

Chapter 3

Law and Marriage, Washington and War

Nixon knew that he would have to compete with others to keep his scholarship. It was good for only one year if he did not get high grades. He worried about it so much—and worked so hard—that he earned the nickname "Gloomy Gus." In 1936, however, he was elected president of the Duke Student Bar Association, and in 1937, he graduated with honors. His whole family drove three thousand miles just to see him graduate, third in his class.

Now Nixon had to think seriously about his future. The Depression still gripped the country, and millions of Americans were hungry, ill-clothed, and out of work. Nixon decided to return to Whittier, where he was hired by the respected law firm of Wingert and Bewley.

Nixon threw himself into community affairs because, as he said, "young lawyers trying to get business for their firms are expected to join local clubs." Within three years he served as president of four organizations and became the youngest member of the Whittier College board of trustees. He also joined the local theater group.

At tryouts for a play called *The Dark Tower*, Dick Nixon met a young business teacher from Whittier High School, who was also trying out for a part. She was tall and graceful, with reddish hair and dark eyes. Just as it had been when Frank met Hannah, Nixon later wrote, "For me, it was a case of love at first sight." Before they had even dated, Dick told Thelma "Pat" Ryan, "Someday I'm going to marry you."

Pat was born in Ely, Nevada, the day before Saint Patrick's Day, 1912. Her father, an Irishman, worked in the silver mines. In 1914, he moved his family from Ely to southern California, where Pat grew up truck farming with her brothers. It was a hard life that became harder when Pat's mother died of cancer. At age fourteen, Pat had to take over household duties. She cooked and sewed, did the washing and ironing, and cleaned house—in addition to working in the fields. Yet she was nearly as active in school as Dick was and also made excellent grades.

At the age of eighteen, Pat lost her father to tuberculosis. She had been taking care of him as Hannah had taken care of Harold. After her father's death, Pat drove an elderly couple clear across the country, making her own car repairs and changing tires along the way. While in New York, she worked with TB patients in a hospital in the Bronx. When she returned to California, she took many jobs to work her way through college, including taking minor parts in Hollywood movies. In 1937, the same year Dick Nixon graduated with honors from Duke, Pat graduated with honors from the University of Southern California. Pat and Dick had many things in common, though they could not have known this when they first met. True to Dick's prophecy—on June 21, 1940, in Riverside, California—he and Pat were married.

Dick Nixon seemed headed for a quiet life as a small-town lawyer and family man. But in 1941, he was offered a job with the government in the Office of Price Administration (OPA). The Nixons moved to Washington, D.C., where he could "observe the working of the government firsthand." Then, on December 7, 1941, Japan bombed the U.S. naval base at Pearl Harbor in Hawaii, and the United States entered World War II.

Nixon was doing a good job at the OPA, and as a Quaker whose religion was against war, he could not be drafted into the armed forces. Nevertheless, he decided to join the navy. In August 1942, he went to Rhode Island for a two-month training course. Upon graduation, he applied for sea duty. Instead, he was sent to a naval air station in Iowa, about as far away from the sea as one could get. Again Nixon applied for sea duty. This time he was assigned to a base in the South Pacific. He was to leave from San Francisco. First, he and Pat drove to Whittier so Dick could say good-bye to his family. Although it troubled them all to see him in uniform, they respected his decision.

Pat found a government job in San Francisco. Dick sailed across the Pacific, a lieutenant j.g. (junior grade).

"I grew up in the Navy," President Nixon later told reporters. He was in charge of getting supplies to the soldiers who were fighting the Japanese and helping with the wounded soldiers. Another officer recalled, "When things got hectic, he never lost his head."

Lieutenant j.g. Richard Nixon in 1942

As the war moved north, Nixon and his men moved with it from island to island. In the Solomon Islands, their unit was bombed twenty-eight nights out of thirty. Nixon would later write of the "terrible reality" of war.

Lieutenant Nixon went out of his way to treat his men well. "I never saw an enlisted man who didn't like him," said a fellow officer. When things were quiet, Nixon taught his men business law. For years afterward, he got letters of gratitude from those who went home after the war and set up their own businesses. It was also during those quiet periods that Nixon's men taught him how to play poker. The Quaker boy from Whittier learned to gamble so well that he rarely lost.

By July 1944, the war in the South Pacific had calmed down. Nixon was ordered to Alameda, in northern California. From there he was sent to Pennsylvania, New York, and Maryland to work on navy contracts. He received an award from the secretary of the navy for saving the navy millions of dollars.

When the war ended in August 1945, Nixon had to think about where he would go and what he would do. In January he would be released from the navy, and Pat was expecting their first child. In September, while living in Baltimore, Nixon received a letter from Herman Perry, a family friend and influential Republican in Whittier. Perry asked if Nixon "would like to be a candidate for Congress on the Republican ticket in 1946." That surprise letter was all Nixon needed to point himself in the direction of politics.

Nixon called Perry to say yes and learned that a Republican "Committee of 100" would be interviewing several possible candidates. The choice would be up to them.

The Committee of 100 represented Republicans—many of them small-business owners—who were unhappy with the government. The country had had a Democratic president since Franklin Delano Roosevelt took office in 1933. The Depression was at its worst then. Roosevelt had started what he called the New Deal to help jobless, homeless, and hungry Americans. A great many new laws were passed to create New Deal agencies and projects.

Harry S. Truman

Upon Roosevelt's death in April 1945, his vice-president, Harry S. Truman, became president. The Depression ended with World War II, but Truman and the Democrats continued Roosevelt's New Deal policies. Republicans did not like to see the government controlling the national economy. They felt the New Deal was no longer needed and was an attack upon private property and free enterprise. They were also alarmed at the confusion that had been created by the new government agencies. Republicans were asking the people of the country if they had "had enough" of Democratic control.

Nixon campaigning in California in February 1946

On November 2, 1945, the Nixons flew from Baltimore to California. Nixon and the other candidates spoke before the Committee of 100. In a brief speech, Nixon called for less government control and more individual freedom. He promised to put on a tough campaign and said he believed the incumbent Democrat, Jerry Voorhis, could be beaten.

The Nixons flew back to Baltimore, and at two o'clock in the morning on November 29, they received a phone call—the Committee of 100 had chosen Nixon. He began his campaign that very morning, writing letters to Republicans in the House of Representatives. He wanted to find out everything he could about his opponent.

Congressman Jerry Voorhis

Jerry Voorhis had won five straight elections in the Twelfth Congressional District (east of Los Angeles) and had served in the House of Representatives for ten years. The idea of a newcomer like Nixon running against Voorhis amused his supporters. Many Republicans would not help Nixon because they felt it was a waste of time and money—Voorhis could not be beaten. Even the Committee of 100 would not donate money to Nixon's campaign until he had won the primary election. Undiscouraged by this lack of support, Pat and Dick had already decided to use half their savings (plus his poker winnings) to finance his first campaign.

In the primaries in June, California voters would decide who would be the Democratic and Republican candidates. If Nixon won the Republican primary, he was sure to run against Voorhis in November in the general election. Nixon was determined to fight—and to win.

Pat plunged in to help run the campaign. On February 17, 1946, the Nixon's first child, Tricia, was born. A few weeks later Pat was back on the job. She worried because they did not have money to buy stamps for mailing Dick's flyers. Some volunteers offered to pass the flyers around, but they turned out to be Democrats who destroyed everything they took.

That same week, Nixon's small office was broken into and the rest of the flyers were destroyed. Nevertheless, Nixon won the Republican primary, and the real battle was on. Jerry Voorhis would find out—too late—the kind of fighter Nixon could be.

To the small-business owners of the Twelfth District, Voorhis represented not only the New Deal, but the threat of Socialism as well. Under Socialism, the state or government controls the economy and most manufacturing and other business. During the Depression some Americans, including Voorhis, became Socialists. They felt that capitalism, or free business enterprise, could no longer work.

Others saw Socialism as not merely a threat to individual freedom but the first step toward Communism, which they viewed as an even greater menace. Under Communism, the government controls all aspects of society—business, farming, education, politics, etc.

Such feelings had their roots in the conflict between the United States and Russia. During World War II, Russia had been America's ally against Hitler and Nazi Germany. Then when the war was over, the Communist government of Russia took over many countries in Eastern Europe, including Hungary, Poland, and East Germany. Americans were feeling strongly anti-Communist.

Nixon followed the national Republican pattern in 1946, branding Voorhis as a tool of the Socialists. He attacked Voorhis for his Socialist and Communist connections, although Voorhis was no longer a Socialist and by no means a Communist.

Nixon kept up his sometimes startling attacks and confused Voorhis during their debates. He showed that he knew Voorhis's congressional voting record better than Voorhis himself.

No polls were taken during the Nixon-Voorhis campaign. During the closing days of the race, the Nixons lived in painful suspense. They had no idea on election day who would win. Not until four o'clock the next morning was it clear that Nixon was the winner, with 65,586 votes to Voorhis's 49,994. The Whittier *News* noted proudly that Richard Nixon was "Whittier's first citizen ever elected to Congress."

Many Republicans were victorious that fall. This would be the only congressional term between 1931 and 1952 that was controlled by Republicans. As a member of the new majority party, Nixon would be able to play a leading role in Congress. Later he admitted that nothing ever matched the excitement of winning his first campaign.

Opposite page: Richard, Pat, and baby Patricia bicycling in Washington, D.C.

Chapter 4

A Postwar Politician

On January 3, 1947, Richard Nixon was sworn in as a member of the United States Congress. He requested assignment to the Labor Committee, and it was through this committee that he met another freshman congressman, John F. (Jack) Kennedy.

Nixon and Kennedy would figure heavily in each other's lives in years to come. They were on opposite sides of labor issues and were opposite in other ways as well. The Democratic Kennedy had come from a rich family in the East and had a degree from Harvard, the school young Nixon could not afford to attend. They respected each other, however, and in a debate over labor problems, neither one could claim a victory.

Nixon was also assigned to the House Un-American Activities Committee (HUAC). This committee was mostly concerned with Communists in the United States. On February 6, 1947, its members called on Gerhard Eisler, an Austrian-born Communist, to answer certain questions. Eisler rudely refused to answer and maintained that the United States was treating him as a "political prisoner."

In his first speech in Congress, on February 18, Nixon said that Eisler came to this country not as a refugee grateful for his opportunity but as an "enemy of our government." He believed that such a "dangerous alien" should not be allowed to enjoy the privileges of our country. It angered some people that Nixon would treat an immigrant so harshly.

Eisler, however, fled to East Germany, and his Communist activities there showed that the young congressman had been right in his suspicions.

In July 1947, Nixon learned that he had been appointed to a select committee to go to Europe. Many countries in Europe were suffering badly from the effects of the war. Secretary of State George Marshall believed that the United States must help these countries, and the committee was selected to study the problem. Not all Americans supported the proposed "Marshall Plan" for giving economic aid to war-torn European countries. Republicans in California's Twelfth District wrote to Nixon before he sailed for Europe and warned him that his support of the plan could hurt the Republican party. Nixon felt he had to make up his own mind.

When the committee landed in Europe, Nixon later wrote, "it was clear that we had come to a continent tottering on the brink of starvation and chaos." He realized that without American aid, millions would die of hunger and disease. In time, Europe would fall to the Communists. He also saw that, no matter what European country Communist leaders lived in, their loyalty was to Russia, not to their own people.

Secretary of State George Marshall

"I had no choice but to vote my conscience," he said, "and then try my hardest to convince my constituents." He not only convinced the voters of the Twelfth District, he became even more popular. In June 1948, he won the votes of both Democrats and Republicans in the primaries. He would be reelected that November without opposition. On July 5, 1948, the Nixons had something else to celebrate—their second daughter, Julie, was born. Then events took a turn that summer that would make Richard Nixon a world figure.

Whittaker Chambers (right) before the House Un-American Activities Committee

On August 3, 1948, Whittaker Chambers, a *Time* magazine editor who had been a Communist, appeared before HUAC. He gave the committee members the names of Communist agents with whom he said he had worked before leaving the Communist party. One of the agents Chambers named was Alger Hiss, a well-known and respected lawyer who had worked in the State Department and had friends in high places. Hiss had helped prepare President Roosevelt for a meeting with the Russian leader Joseph Stalin in 1945; in 1948, he was president of the Carnegie Endowment for International Peace. Hiss was outraged at the charges made against him and demanded to appear before HUAC to deny them.

Former State Department employee Alger Hiss

Alger Hiss said he had "never known a man named Whittaker Chambers." He spoke eloquently in his own defense and was applauded by many HUAC members and newspapermen who were present. It would have been much easier for Nixon to let the matter drop, as most HUAC members wanted to do. But something about the way Hiss spoke bothered him. Either Chambers or Hiss was lying, and Nixon was determined to find out which one. He met with Chambers several times and questioned him further. Nixon was warned by older congressmen to stop, but he wrote to Hannah: "Mother, I think Hiss is lying. Until I know the truth, I've got to stick it out."

Nixon and HUAC chief investigator Robert Stripling examine the "pumpkin papers."

Eventually, Alger Hiss confessed that he may have known Chambers under another name. Then, in December, Chambers gave the committee some rolls of microfilm that he had been hiding in a hollowed-out pumpkin. The famous "pumpkin papers" were copies of State Department papers, many of which appeared to have been copied on Hiss's typewriter. This was enough to convince a jury that Hiss was a Communist agent who had stolen top secret information from the United States government and that he had lied under oath. Hiss was sentenced to five years in jail. It was a personal victory for Richard Nixon.

Nixon scans the headlines after a federal grand jury found Hiss guilty of perjury.

Unfortunately for the Republicans, Harry Truman was elected to the presidency that fall, and the Democrats regained their congressional majority. In spite of Nixon's overwhelming reelection, as a minority member of Congress he could no longer play a leading role. He began to look to the 1950 elections. Many Californians thought he should run for the Senate, and Nixon agreed. There were a million more registered Democrats in California than Republicans, but Nixon called for a "fighting, rocking, socking campaign." In 1950, he got his wish.

Nixon's opponent was Helen Gahagan Douglas, wife of the movie star Melvyn Douglas and a congresswoman who had also been an actress. Before the June primaries, Douglas and other Democrats had battled among themselves for the Democratic nomination. The Democratic candidate who then held the Senate seat dropped out of the race, saying he was too ill to fight "the vicious and unethical" campaign Helen Douglas had launched against him. Another candidate accused Mrs. Douglas of being pro-Communist, although she was not.

When Nixon won the Republican nomination that June and Douglas gained the Democratic nomination, the fight was on. Douglas made the foolish charge that Nixon was part of a pro-Communist group. Nixon countered by accusing her of being a "pinko." ("Pinko" meant someone who favored Communism.) Nixon headquarters printed fact sheets about Douglas on pink paper. These somewhat misleading "pink sheets" hurt Douglas. She, in turn, called Nixon "tricky Dick" and said many things about him that were not true. Nixon worried that he would lose, so he fought twice as hard. He received some help from strange quarters.

One day Jack Kennedy came to Nixon's office and handed him an envelope. "Dick, I know you're in for a pretty rough campaign," he said, "and my father wanted to help out." The two congressmen chatted for a while, and after Kennedy left, Nixon opened the envelope. It contained a $1,000 campaign contribution. Even though the Kennedys were Democrats, they did not want to see Douglas elected.

Helen Gahagan Douglas votes in the primaries.

In the November general elections, Nixon won by a margin of 680,000 votes. This was the biggest win of any senator that year. Twice Nixon had been elected to serve a two-year term in the House of Representatives. Now he was elected to serve a six-year term in the Senate. He served only two of those six years, however. In the election of 1952, as General Eisenhower's running mate, Richard Nixon was swept into the second highest office in the land.

Chapter 5

Vice-President and
World Traveler

A vice-president has few duties and can easily be forgotten in his role as backup to the president. Nixon, however, was to play a greater role in governing the nation than had any previous vice-president.

By August 1949, China had fallen to the Communist "Red Chinese." In September, Americans were alarmed to learn that Russia had exploded an atomic bomb. In 1950, Communist forces invaded the Republic of Korea, and Americans found themselves at war with Communism on the continent of Asia.

Anti-Communist feelings ran so high in the early 1950s that many innocent people were accused of being spies. One senator, Republican Joseph McCarthy of Wisconsin, became violent and irresponsible in accusing certain Americans of being disloyal. Eisenhower asked Nixon to try to moderate McCarthy's anti-Communist crusade. For a while, Nixon was able to curb McCarthy, whose behavior was an embarrassment to Republicans. By 1954, however, McCarthy's attacks had become so reckless that he was condemned by the Senate. "McCarthyism" became a word used to describe unfounded accusations that make the accused person seem guilty.

During his vice-presidency, Nixon's childhood dream of traveling to faraway places came true beyond his wildest imagining. In his eight years as vice-president (he and Ike would be reelected in 1956), Nixon made nine overseas trips, visiting sixty-one countries on almost every continent, and covering almost 160,000 miles.

The young vice-president traveled as an official visitor and received a royal welcome wherever he went. Still, he insisted on meeting with common, ordinary people—students, laborers, businessmen. Pat—who accompanied Dick—visited schools, hospitals, and orphanages. This shocked some officials, but the Nixons were determined to learn about the people of other countries, not just their leaders. "Eisenhower used to think of us as a team," Nixon later wrote, "and so did I."

Nixon took his first trip as vice-president, at Eisenhower's request, to Asia in 1953. Many of the Asian nations had been colonies of European countries for some time. Asians wanted the freedom to govern themselves, but Nixon saw the danger of Communist takeovers in nations that might be given independence.

As Nixon feared, in March 1954, Communist soldiers attacked a French fort at Dien Bien Phu in Vietnam. Eisenhower sent a small number of military advisers to Vietnam to help France fight the Communists. But in May, the French soldiers were defeated. In July, at a peace conference in Geneva, Switzerland, Vietnam was divided into two countries, Communist North Vietnam and non-Communist South Vietnam. The Korean War had ended with Korea similarly divided into two nations. Eisenhower and

President Eisenhower at Fitzsimons Army Hospital, Denver, Colorado

Nixon did not approve of letting the Communists have half of Vietnam. They feared a "domino effect"—other Asian countries would fall if Vietnam fell to the Communists. So the United States did not sign the peace agreement. This was the beginning of American involvement in the long and bitter Vietnam War, a war that Nixon—as president—would end nearly twenty years later.

The possibility of Nixon becoming president seemed close when, on September 24, 1955, Eisenhower suffered a severe heart attack. For almost two months, while Ike was in the hospital, Nixon had to perform many of the president's duties. As close as he was to the highest position of power, Nixon did not try to advance himself personally. Secretary of State John Foster Dulles praised Nixon for conducting himself "superbly" during a difficult time.

The vice-president visits his parents in Whittier in February 1954.

Ike felt well enough in 1956 to run again. But Frank Nixon did not live to see his son and Ike reelected. He died in Whittier during the campaign, with Richard by his side.

Meanwhile, in central Europe, the Hungarian people rebelled against their Communist government. With tanks and armed soldiers, the Russian Communists brutally crushed the rebellion. Over 100,000 freedom fighters had to flee their homes in Hungary.

In December 1956, Eisenhower sent Nixon to Austria to look into the problem of the Hungarian refugees there and to show American support for their cause. Nixon wanted to see the dangerous border where the refugees crossed over from Communist Europe into free Europe. Traveling in the back of a large hay wagon pulled by a tractor, he could see the guard towers, the searchlights, and the dogs patrolling along the barbed wire. And he saw the nightmarish fence designed to keep people *in* rather than out.

The Nixons with Goa devil dancers in Liberia during their African tour

In the spring of 1957, Eisenhower sent Nixon to Africa to meet with leaders of the African nations. While in Ghana at an independence celebration, Nixon met another American visitor, Reverend Martin Luther King, Jr., the civil rights leader. Nixon invited Dr. King to meet with him in Washington. After their return to the United States, the two men met again and discussed Nixon's efforts to promote a civil rights bill. Nixon was deeply impressed by Dr. King. They agreed that equal opportunity for all should be gained by peaceful rather than by violent means. King later wrote to Nixon: ". . . how deeply grateful we are to you for your assiduous labor and dauntless courage in seeking to make the Civil Rights Bill a reality."

In the fall of 1957, Americans faced a crisis in race relations. Governor Orval Faubus of Arkansas defied a court order to integrate Little Rock Central High School, which black students were not allowed to attend. Nixon strongly supported Eisenhower when the president sent federal troops to enforce the order. The Nixons' two daughters attended an integrated school, and Richard Nixon firmly believed in integration.

On October 4, 1957, Russia fired into orbit the world's first artificial satellite, *Sputnik*. This stunning technological feat created another crisis for Americans, who saw the Russian lead in rocketry as a threat to national security. The nation called for an all-out effort to regain its technical superiority, and the "space race" was launched.

Then, on November 25, 1957, Eisenhower suffered a stroke. His chief of staff, Sherman Adams, told Nixon, "You may be president in twenty-four hours." Once again, Nixon took over many of the presidential duties. But Ike proved Adams wrong. When he returned to the White House, Eisenhower wrote a four-page letter to Nixon granting him the power to act as president in any future emergency. It was a tremendous vote of confidence.

In 1958, Eisenhower asked Nixon to visit South America. The Central Intelligence Agency (CIA) warned Nixon that Communists there might stage demonstrations against him. Communists opposed the United States' role in supporting the policies of several South American dictators. However, the Communist party was suppressed in most South American countries. Nixon believed the trip would be uneventful.

Above: Arkansas governor Orval Faubus making a television appeal for segregation
Below: National Guardsmen turn a black student away from Little Rock Central High.

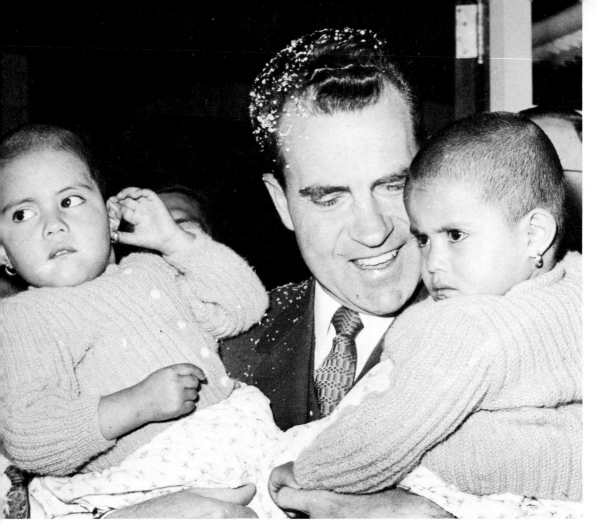

Nixon at a U.S. health center in La Paz, Bolivia, during his South American tour

The South American trip got off to a good start, with the vice-president and his wife well received in Uruguay, Argentina, Paraguay, and Bolivia. Any demonstrations in these countries were mild. But in Lima, Peru, the travelers were greeted with reports that "Latin-American Communists have orders to play it tough from here on with Vice President Nixon. . . ." Nixon refused to cancel his visit, and while Pat stayed back at their hotel, he was shouted at and spat upon by a violent crowd in the streets of Lima.

Youngsters in Caracas take part in an anti-Nixon demonstration.

Matters grew worse when the Nixons reached Venezuela. From the moment they arrived in the capital of Caracas, their lives were in danger. At the airport terminal, spit and garbage rained down upon them. When they finally got into their cars and began the motorcade, a mob threw rocks at them, smashed the windshield of Nixon's car, and even tried to turn it over. Pat was in the car behind her husband. Nixon ordered the motorcade away from the planned route. He learned later that homemade bombs had been waiting for him.

In Washington, President Eisenhower feared for the lives of the Nixons and those who accompanied them. He put American military forces on alert. The Nixons remained dignified and cool-headed throughout the incident, but they could hardly wait to get home to Tricia and Julie.

Nixon believed that the United States needed to work with the Latin American peoples "in moving toward democracy, toward freedom, toward economic progress." In Cuba, ninety miles off the coast of Florida, it was already too late.

On New Year's Day, 1959, Fidel Castro overthrew the non-Communist dictator, President Fulgencio Batista. Many Americans cheered, not realizing that Castro was a Communist who would soon try to bring Russian nuclear missiles to Cuba. The most frightening aspect of this for many Americans was that the missiles would be positioned within striking distance of Washington, D.C.

On July 22, 1959, Nixon flew to Moscow to open the first United States Exhibition ever held in Russia. He met with the Russian premier, Nikita Khrushchev, whose violent temper and rude outbursts were well known. At the exhibition, the two men held their now-famous "Kitchen Debate" in a model kitchen filled with the latest American gadgets.

Nixon put forth a positive view of American life. He did not back down when Khrushchev shouted or attacked his views. Americans, watching them on television, saw Nixon as the man who stood up to Khrushchev—and made the Russian "bear" smile.

Nixon and Soviet premier Nikita Khrushchev

After touring Russia, the Nixons visited Poland. Though Poland was ruled by a Communist government, the Polish people turned out in huge numbers to shower the Nixons not with stones but with flowers. A quarter of a million people gathered along the fifteen miles leading to Warsaw, cheering the Nixons, who represented America and freedom. Several times Vice-President Nixon got out of his car to shake hands with the people. Many of them wept. The Nixons would never forget this demonstration that showed how much the United States meant to Eastern Europe.

Chapter 6

Victories and Defeats

In 1960, Eisenhower's second term was drawing to a close. By law, he could not run again. The Republicans chose Richard Nixon to be their presidential candidate in that year's election, and the Democrats nominated John F. Kennedy. The two congressmen had come a long way since their first terms in the Senate.

Nixon had a clear advantage over Kennedy. He had experience in performing presidential duties. He was well known and respected for his visits to foreign countries and meetings with their leaders. But television was more important in 1960 than in any previous election year. It brought the candidates into homes all over America. Kennedy's youthful appearance, his warm smile, and his sense of humor appealed to the American public. And he, like Nixon, was skilled in debate. In a televised campaign debate, in spite of Nixon's knowledge and experience, Kennedy clearly emerged the winner.

Kennedy also had his father's wealth to back him, plus the fact that Democrats throughout the country outnumbered Republicans. Still, the race was a close one. Nobody was sure who would win. It might have been Richard Nixon, but last-minute votes from Illinois and Texas gave the presidency to Kennedy.

Opposite page: Nixon on the night
of his presidential nomination

Many people believed that those last votes were not honest. Eisenhower and others urged Nixon to demand a recount. But Nixon refused, believing it would divide the country for many months and hurt America's image abroad. He felt strongly that whoever was president must be able to deal with the world from a strong position. He would not weaken President Kennedy by contesting the election results.

The Nixons decided to return to California, where the former vice-president practiced law for a short time. In the 1962 California elections, Nixon ran for governor. Many Republicans, including Eisenhower, considered it Nixon's duty to seek this prominent office. His heart was not in the campaign, however, and he lost to the Democratic incumbent, Edmund G. "Pat" Brown. This second defeat, he said, was "like being bitten by a mosquito after being bitten by a snake."

Nixon met with reporters after the election and shocked them by saying, "You won't have Nixon to kick around anymore, because, gentlemen, this is my last press conference." A week later, *Time* magazine declared, "Barring a miracle, [Nixon's] political career ended last week."

In 1963, the Nixons moved to New York, where Dick Nixon joined a law practice with international clients. This allowed him to continue to travel the world and study other countries.

On November 22, 1963, on his return to New York from a business trip to Dallas, Texas, Nixon heard terrible news: President Kennedy, who was visiting Dallas, had been shot. Kennedy's vice-president, Lyndon Johnson, was sworn in as the new president of the United States. The country went into mourning.

In 1964, Lyndon Johnson was elected to continue as president. He ran against Barry Goldwater, a Republican senator from Arizona, and won by a landslide. It was clear to Nixon that the Republican party was in trouble. Different factions were quarreling bitterly and had to be pulled together if the party was going to stay alive. Nixon felt that he must pitch in and do whatever he could, a decision that marked the beginning of his amazing political comeback.

By now, the United States had become deeply involved in the war in Vietnam. For the first time in history, people could see the horrors of war on television in their own living rooms.

Many Americans were against U.S. involvement in Vietnam. Furthermore, they blamed President Johnson for escalating the conflict. Outraged citizens held demonstrations to protest the war, and some of these became violent. Near the end of his term, Johnson announced that he would not run for president again.

The election year 1968 brought even more violence to America. In April, the Reverend Martin Luther King, Jr., the peaceful leader of the civil rights movement, was shot to death. When the news became public, riots broke out in black sections of cities across the country.

On June 5, 1968, Robert Kennedy, Jack Kennedy's brother, won the Democratic nomination for president in the California primary. That same evening, Kennedy was gunned down by an assassin and died the next morning.

**Above: Jacqueline Kennedy, with the slain president John Kennedy's brothers
Ted and Robert and children Caroline and John, Jr., at Kennedy's funeral
Below: Marines in Vietnam's demilitarized zone, carrying an injured buddy**

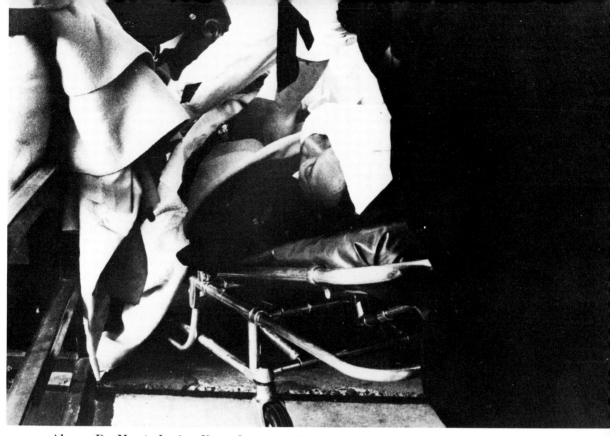

Above: Dr. Martin Luther King, Jr., mortally wounded in his Memphis motel
Below: Robert Kennedy, shot by an assassin in Los Angeles after his presidential nomination

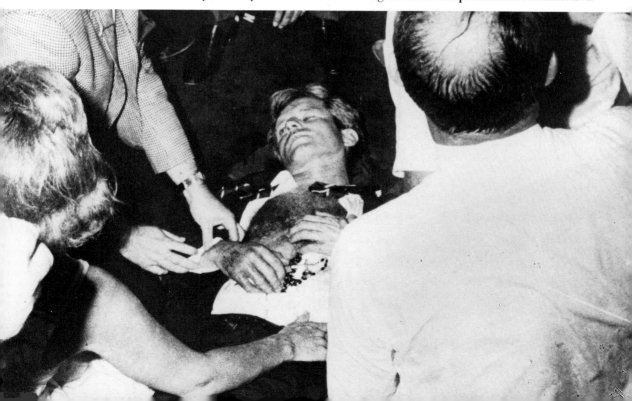

Antiwar demonstrators during the 1968 Democratic national convention in Chicago

In August 1968, at the Democratic national convention in Chicago, Illinois, Johnson's vice-president, Hubert Humphrey, was nominated to run for president. Outside in the streets, violence erupted between antiwar demonstrators and the Chicago police. Bottles, sticks, and stones flew through the air as the police used clubs and tear gas to battle the mob. Nixon later wrote, "Like millions of other Americans watching television that night, I did not want to believe my eyes."

By contrast, the Republican national convention in Miami, Florida, was remarkably peaceful. Richard Nixon, who had helped to bring the Republican party together, was nominated as the 1968 Republican presidential candidate. On election day in November, the polls showed that

Nixon escorts Julie at New York's Marble Collegiate Church on her wedding day.

Nixon and Humphrey were running neck and neck. Nixon's victory was a narrow one, but the "miracle" had happened. Unfortunately, Hannah Nixon did not live to see her son become president of the United States. She had died the year before at the age of eighty-two.

On December 22, 1968, Julie Nixon and Dwight David Eisenhower II, Ike's grandson, were married. Twenty-nine days later, Richard Nixon took the oath of office. As Julie later wrote, at her father's inauguration day parade there were 250,000 happily cheering people. There were also hundreds of demonstrators throwing sticks, rocks, empty beer cans, and homemade smoke bombs. It was "a sobering reminder of the deep discontent in the country and of the urgent need for action."

Nixon mingles with combat troops of the First Infantry Division in South Vietnam.

Nixon wanted the Vietnam War to end as much as any other American did. But he wanted to end it "honorably," with South Vietnam a free country. In June 1969 he announced a policy called "Vietnamization." This included increased training of South Vietnamese soldiers to fight their own war and a gradual reduction of U.S. troops in Vietnam.

That same year, Nixon directed the Air Force to extend its bombing raids into Cambodia to hit suspected enemy bases. Then in April 1970, he ordered an invasion of Cambodia to clear out any North Vietnamese supply bases there. Antiwar protesters demonstrated against this widening of the war and called for peace talks.

A Kent State University student, wounded by Ohio National Guardsmen

In May 1970, at Kent State University in Ohio, students protesting the Cambodian invasion damaged several college buildings. The Ohio National Guard was called out to handle the disturbance. At one point, some of the guardsmen suddenly opened fire upon a group of student demonstrators. Tragically, four students were killed and nine were injured. In response, demonstrations broke out on hundreds of other college campuses.

Despite the bombings in Cambodia, the war did not end. Nixon and his national security adviser, Henry Kissinger, tried to negotiate a peace treaty with the North Vietnamese, but the peace talks bogged down. Finally, in January 1973, a cease-fire agreement was signed, and Nixon withdrew all American troops.

Unfortunately, North and South Vietnam continued to fight, and eventually North Vietnamese forces overran the country. South Vietnam surrendered in April 1975. Though Nixon had achieved a peace agreement, the legacy of the Vietnam era continued to affect the nation. For the first time in its history, the United States had lost a war.

During President Nixon's first term, he took several steps to improve conditions for many people in the United States. Strong new anticrime laws were passed, as he had promised. The military draft was reduced and then eliminated. Taxes were cut, a measure that helped the average American family.

Nixon also made progress in the areas of civil rights and equal opportunities for women. He proposed dramatic new steps in welfare reform, health care, and environmental programs. It was difficult at times to push some of his policies through because he faced opposition from a Democratic Congress. Perhaps most importantly, Nixon made great strides in foreign relations.

Ever since China had been taken over by the Communists, the United States had had no relations with this huge Asian country. Nixon believed such diplomatic stalemates were dangerous and unhealthy. As president, he opened the door for the first exchanges with China in twenty-one years. In October 1971, he supported Communist China's admission to the United Nations. In February 1972, the Nixons visited China for seven days. It was a "week that changed the world" by peacefully bringing together the leaders of two powerful and very different countries.

Above: Nixon and Chinese premier Chou En-lai share a toast in the Great Hall of the People in Peking, February 1972.   Below: Nixon and Soviet leader Leonid Brezhnev after signing their 1974 arms limitation agreement

The Nixons visited Russia again in 1972. Khrushchev had died and Leonid Brezhnev was the new Russian leader. At this time, Russia was building large numbers of nuclear missiles. The United States military urged Nixon to spend billions of dollars to make more American missiles to beat the Russians in an arms race. Instead, Nixon talked to Brezhnev and other Russian leaders about limiting both countries' buildup of arms.

Out of these talks came the first Strategic Arms Limitation Treaty, known as the SALT agreement. The limiting of arms by both the United States and Russia would not only save the United States money, but it would make the world safer for almost a decade.

On June 13, 1971 (the day after Tricia Nixon was married to Edward Cox), the *New York Times* ran a story that shocked the president and his staff. The *Times* had been given the so-called Pentagon Papers, which included government foreign policy secrets.

Daniel Ellsberg, a former Pentagon aide in the United States Department of Defense, had taken these papers and given them to the press. The papers revealed that Nixon and the Pentagon had not told Congress the truth about how the Vietnam War was going and about U.S. involvement in it.

The Pentagon Papers also disclosed many other facts that made it more difficult for Nixon to pursue his foreign policy. Nixon ordered his staff to find out what other secrets Ellsberg might reveal.

By fall, the CIA reported that the American government was experiencing the worst outbreak of "news leaks" in nearly twenty years. (A news leak occurs when someone gives information to the media without the knowledge or permission of those in charge of the government.) These leaks were highly damaging to the United States' relations with other countries.

President Nixon and Henry Kissinger were still involved in peace talks with North Vietnam. When their private conversations appeared in newspapers all over the country, their work was greatly undermined. J. Edgar Hoover, director of the Federal Bureau of Investigation (FBI), suggested to Nixon that he might want to do what Presidents Roosevelt, Kennedy, and Johnson had done: "tap" the telephone conversations of people working for him to try and find out who was leaking information to the news media.

As he was about to leave office, President Johnson had shown Nixon some of his secret wiretapping system. Johnson also urged Nixon to tape all his White House conversations for his memoirs. Nevertheless, when Nixon took office, he had Johnson's wiretapping system removed from the White House.

In the months to come, President Nixon decided to install new equipment. He also had microphones hidden in a number of White House offices to record conversations that he would be having with others. The presidents before him had done the same thing, though not nearly as extensively as Nixon—nor with such tragic results. In a few years, Nixon's "White House tapes" would contribute to his downfall in what would be known as the Watergate affair.

Chapter 7

Four More Years?

In 1972, the Republicans nominated Richard Nixon to run for a second term as president. The vote was an overwhelming 1,347 to 1. Nixon's supporters chanted enthusiastically, "Four more years! Four more years!"

The president had accomplished a great deal at home and abroad, and the majority of Americans believed he was doing a good job. The Democratic candidate, George McGovern, seemed to appeal to a small minority. President Nixon was sure to be reelected.

During the summer of 1972, five men were arrested for breaking into the Democratic National Headquarters in Washington's Watergate Hotel. Nixon read about the Watergate break-in in a copy of the *Miami Herald* newspaper while he was vacationing in the Bahamas. It seemed that the men were trying to "bug" the Democratic offices by planting listening devices in the rooms. Later Nixon learned that one of them was working for the Committee to Re-Elect President Nixon. He could not understand why anyone on the committee would do this.

President Nixon put the Watergate break-in out of his mind. He had far more important things to think about, such as the war in Vietnam. His Democratic opponent, George McGovern, believed the United States should pull out of the war immediately. Nixon felt this would be wrong and favored a gradual withdrawal.

Opposite page: Nixon giving his farewell
speech after resigning the presidency

77

Watergate stories continued to appear in the news. Democrats were outraged by the incident and other "tricks" that had been played on them. Yet, at the same time, Republican committee rooms had been bugged by McGovern's people. There were also many reports of violence during the campaign. By election day, Nixon headquarters in Texas, Ohio, Minnesota, Arizona, and California had been either bombed, burned, or broken into and their flyers destroyed. These incidents made Watergate, by itself, seem insignificant to the president.

On September 15, 1972, formal charges—or indictments—were brought against seven people who had been involved in the Watergate break-in. Over three hundred FBI agents had talked to some 1,500 people and concluded that no one in the White House was involved. In October, however, the *Washington Post* ran stories that indicated otherwise. Nixon's closest aides, the newspaper suggested, were behind the break-in. They were also involved in "dirty tricks" played on the Democrats.

Watergate was becoming an open wound that was not about to heal. It did not affect voters in the November general elections, however. Nixon easily won and would remain in the White House, though not for four more years.

President Nixon's second inauguration, on January 20, 1973, took place three days before the announcement of a cease-fire in Vietnam. The president spoke from the east front of the Capitol. "As we meet here today," he said, "we stand at the threshold of a new era of peace in the world."

Former prisoner of war Robert Strimm is greeted by his family on his return.

In February 1973, the first prisoners of war returned home from Vietnam. Millions of Americans watched on television as these pitifully thin and feeble men arrived in the United States. Some hobbled on crutches, while others fell to their knees to kiss the ground of the country they loved. The former prisoners praised the president and thanked him for bringing them home.

Nixon was nowhere near as popular with the Democrats in Congress, however. In March 1973, Democratic senators voted to begin an investigation of the 1972 Republican campaign and the Watergate break-in. They were determined to bring to light any wrongdoing on the part of Richard Nixon, his cabinet, and his aides.

The Senate Watergate hearings brought panic to the people surrounding the president. Gradually Nixon learned how deeply involved some of his trusted aides had been in the crimes being investigated. The president, trying to protect himself and his aides, was already involved in illegal "cover-up" activities. He, and others in the White House, had violated the law by obstructing justice—hiding facts from those who were investigating the crimes. In time, Nixon would be forced to give all his private tapes to the investigators.

Another break-in had occurred, in 1971, in the office of Daniel Ellsberg's psychiatrist. The "burglars" wanted to find incriminating information about Ellsberg. Nixon and his aides would be blamed for this break-in as well. Ellsberg, on trial for giving the Pentagon Papers to the media, was set free since some of the evidence against him had been obtained, illegally, in the break-in.

The Watergate investigations continued, probing the involvement of White House staff and cabinet members in the cover-up and other illegal activities. The president was severely attacked in newspapers and on television. Many of his accomplishments were overshadowed by the findings of the investigation. There was even talk of impeaching him. Under the United States Constitution, Congress could place the president on trial, and with a two-thirds vote in the Senate, he could be removed from office.

To make matters worse, Nixon's vice-president, Spiro Agnew, was in trouble. Agnew, a former governor of Maryland, was accused of having taken bribes from people doing business with the state of Maryland. He was also

Nixon and Gerald Ford after Ford's vice-presidential nomination

accused of not paying income taxes on the money he received. On October 10, 1973, Agnew announced that he was resigning his office. Two days later, President Nixon nominated Gerald R. Ford, the House minority leader and a congressman from Michigan, to replace Agnew. In December, Congress approved the nomination.

In October of that year, Egypt and Syria launched a surprise attack against Israel. Nixon startled the nation by putting America's armed forces on alert. Some people said he was just trying to take attention away from Watergate, but that was far from the case. President Nixon sent American airplanes with much-needed supplies to Israel to keep it from being overrun. After a cease-fire was arranged in the Middle East, Nixon worked hard to bring the warring countries together in peace.

Senator Sam Ervin (center), chairman of the Watergate Investigating Committee

The attacks upon Nixon continued and seriously weakened his presidency. It seemed as if every day brought fresh charges against the president and his administration. Even though some of the charges would prove to be false, Nixon looked worse and worse in the eyes of many Americans. Some people called for his removal from office, while others supported him and urged the president not to give up.

The Nixons in Cairo, Egypt, with President and Mrs. Anwar Sadat

In June 1974, Nixon made a successful trip to the Middle East, where he met with leaders of the countries who had fought on both sides of the war. He also made another visit to Russia. Afterwards, the president wrote in his diary that the trip had "put the whole Watergate business into perspective" for him. It seemed to him that "the terrible battering" his administration had taken was "really pygmy-sized when compared to what we have done and what we can do in the future . . . for peace in the world. . . ."

But the battering continued. By August, almost all of the president's top aides were gone. Many had been forced to resign, and some were charged with crimes for which they would go to jail. Members of the House of Representatives were preparing formal charges of impeachment against the president.

Nixon had refused to weaken Kennedy's presidency by challenging the vote count in 1960. Now, in 1974, his own presidency had been so seriously challenged that it was weakened beyond repair. "The presidency is bigger than any man . . . ," he said, "bigger than any individual president. . . ." He could not stay on to fight back—it would only hurt the country.

On August 9, 1974, Richard Nixon resigned from office, the first president to do so. Pat and the girls and their husbands stood by him, as they had through the long ordeal. Foreign leaders who had trusted and admired President Nixon could not understand how this tragedy had happened. The leaders of England, France, Israel, and many other countries expressed disbelief and dismay.

During Nixon's trip to Russia in June 1974, the Russian leader Leonid Brezhnev had put his arm around the president and said, "We want every Russian and every American to be friends that talk to each other as you and I are talking to each other here. . . ." President Nixon might have been able to make further strides toward world peace if there had not been a Watergate.

Richard Nixon's resignation marked the end of his presidency and the beginning of a new way of life—outside the rough and tumble of politics.

Opposite page: Nixon boarding a helicopter after his resignation as president

Chapter 8

After Watergate

In 1978, Richard Nixon's *Memoirs*, a book he had written about his life, was published. In it he recalled his departure from the White House: "The crowd, covering the lawn, spilling out onto the balconies, leaning out of the windows. Silent, waving, crying. . . . I raised my arms in a final salute. I smiled. I waved goodbye."

The Nixons flew to California, where another crowd awaited them. Many people were holding small American flags, and some wept as the Nixons emerged from the plane. Nixon began to shake hands with people, and the crowd started singing "God Bless America." A voice called out, "Whittier's still for you, Dick." But he knew that his political life was over.

The Nixons retired to their home in San Clemente, where Richard Nixon would write in his *Memoirs*:

Life in the White House is active and intense. For one thing, it is a city home and there is always the sense and sound of traffic outside. Sometimes there would be the sound of demonstrations. Inside, it often seemed as if there were never any real privacy as the household staff went about their work, and in the basement the kitchens were constantly bustling with preparations for the steady stream of breakfasts, luncheons, teas, receptions, and official dinners.

Now their life in San Clemente was slow and quiet.

Nixon gets pointers on how to spin the ball from Harlem Globetrotters on the occasion of his 1986 Public Service Award for contributions to health and fitness in America.

In Washington, the Watergate investigations continued. But in September 1974, President Gerald Ford—who had been Nixon's vice-president—granted him a full and unconditional pardon for whatever wrongs he may have committed while in office.

The following month, Nixon became ill and had a close brush with death. For two days, while he lay in the hospital, his family feared that they might lose him. But Richard Nixon had more work to do. He recovered from his illness and went on writing, not only about his life but about world affairs. He felt he must share his knowledge and experience with others. This would be his way of continuing to fight for what he believed in and for "the cause of peace and freedom."

In October 1981, the Nixons moved to Saddle River, New Jersey. In 1986, an interviewer asked the thirty-seventh president how he thought he would be rated by future generations. "Without the Watergate episode I would be rated, I should think, rather high," he said. "But with it, it depends on who's doing the rating."

In the calmer light of history, future generations will be able to weigh Richard Nixon's accomplishments against the mistakes revealed by Watergate. Only then will people gain an objective view of this capable yet complex man and the troubled times in which he governed.

Chronology of American History

(Shaded area covers events in Richard Nixon's lifetime.)

About A.D. 982 — Eric the Red, born in Norway, reaches Greenland in one of the first European voyages to North America.

About 985 — Eric the Red brings settlers from Iceland to Greenland.

About 1000 — Leif Ericson (Eric the Red's son) leads what is thought to be the first European expedition to mainland North America; Leif probably lands in Canada.

1492 — Christopher Columbus, seeking a sea route from Spain to the Far East, discovers the New World.

1497 — John Cabot reaches Canada in the first English voyage to North America.

1513 — Ponce de Léon explores Florida in search of the fabled Fountain of Youth.

1519-1521 — Hernando Cortés of Spain conquers Mexico.

1534 — French explorers led by Jacques Cartier enter the Gulf of St. Lawrence in Canada.

1540 — Spanish explorer Francisco Coronado begins exploring the American Southwest, seeking the riches of the mythical Seven Cities of Cibola.

1565 — St. Augustine, Florida, the first permanent European town in what is now the United States, is founded by the Spanish.

1607 — Jamestown, Virginia, is founded, the first permanent English town in the present-day U.S.

1608 — Frenchman Samuel de Champlain founds the village of Quebec, Canada.

1609 — Henry Hudson explores the eastern coast of present-day U.S. for the Netherlands; the Dutch then claim parts of New York, New Jersey, Delaware, and Connecticut and name the area New Netherland.

1619 — The English colonies' first shipment of black slaves arrives in Jamestown.

1620 — English Pilgrims found Massachusetts' first permanent town at Plymouth.

1621 — Massachusetts Pilgrims and Indians hold the famous first Thanksgiving feast in colonial America.

1623 — Colonization of New Hampshire is begun by the English.

1624 — Colonization of present-day New York State is begun by the Dutch at Fort Orange (Albany).

1625 — The Dutch start building New Amsterdam (now New York City).

1630 — The town of Boston, Massachusetts, is founded by the English Puritans.

1633 — Colonization of Connecticut is begun by the English.

1634 — Colonization of Maryland is begun by the English.

1636 — Harvard, the colonies' first college, is founded in Massachusetts. Rhode Island colonization begins when Englishman Roger Williams founds Providence.

1638 — Delaware colonization begins when Swedish people build Fort Christina at present-day Wilmington.

1640 — Stephen Daye of Cambridge, Massachusetts prints *The Bay Psalm Book*, the first English-language book published in what is now the U.S.

1643 — Swedish settlers begin colonizing Pennsylvania.

About 1650 — North Carolina is colonized by Virginia settlers.

1660 — New Jersey colonization is begun by the Dutch at present-day Jersey City.

1670 — South Carolina colonization is begun by the English near Charleston.

1673 — Jacques Marquette and Louis Jolliet explore the upper Mississippi River for France.

1682—Philadelphia, Pennsylvania, is settled. La Salle explores Mississippi River all the way to its mouth in Louisiana and claims the whole Mississippi Valley for France.

1693—College of William and Mary is founded in Williamsburg, Virginia.

1700—Colonial population is about 250,000.

1703—Benjamin Franklin is born in Boston.

1732—George Washington, first president of the U.S., is born in Westmoreland County, Virginia.

1733—James Oglethorpe founds Savannah, Georgia; Georgia is established as the thirteenth colony.

1735—John Adams, second president of the U.S., is born in Braintree, Massachusetts.

1737—William Byrd founds Richmond, Virginia.

1738—British troops are sent to Georgia over border dispute with Spain.

1739—Black insurrection takes place in South Carolina.

1740—English Parliament passes act allowing naturalization of immigrants to American colonies after seven-year residence.

1743—Thomas Jefferson, third president of the U.S., is born in Albemarle County, Virginia. Benjamin Franklin retires at age thirty-seven to devote himself to scientific inquiries and public service.

1744—King George's War begins; France joins war effort against England.

1745—During King George's War, France raids settlements in Maine and New York.

1747—Classes begin at Princeton College in New Jersey.

1748—The Treaty of Aix-la-Chapelle concludes King George's War.

1749—Parliament legally recognizes slavery in colonies and the inauguration of the plantation system in the South. George Washington becomes the surveyor for Culpepper County in Virginia.

1750—Thomas Walker passes through and names Cumberland Gap on his way toward Kentucky region. Colonial population is about 1,200,000.

1751—James Madison, fourth president of the U.S., is born in Port Conway, Virginia. English Parliament passes Currency Act, banning New England colonies from issuing paper money. George Washington travels to Barbados.

1752—Pennsylvania Hospital, the first general hospital in the colonies, is founded in Philadelphia. Benjamin Franklin uses a kite in a thunderstorm to demonstrate that lightning is a form of electricity.

1753—George Washington delivers command from Virginia Lieutenant Governor Dinwiddie that the French withdraw from the Ohio River Valley; French disregard the demand. Colonial population is about 1,328,000.

1754—French and Indian War begins (extends to Europe as the Seven Years' War). Washington surrenders at Fort Necessity.

1755—French and Indians ambush General Braddock. Washington becomes commander of Virginia troops.

1756—England declares war on France.

1758—James Monroe, fifth president of the U.S., is born in Westmoreland County, Virginia.

1759—Cherokee Indian war begins in southern colonies; hostilities extend to 1761. George Washington marries Martha Dandridge Custis.

1760—George III becomes king of England. Colonial population is about 1,600,000.

1762—England declares war on Spain.

1763—Treaty of Paris concludes the French and Indian War and the Seven Years' War. England gains Canada and most other French lands east of the Mississippi River.

1764—British pass the Sugar Act to gain tax money from the colonists. The issue of taxation without representation is first introduced in Boston. John Adams marries Abigail Smith.

1765—Stamp Act goes into effect in the colonies. Business virtually stops as almost all colonists refuse to use the stamps.

1766—British repeal the Stamp Act.

1767—John Quincy Adams, sixth president of the U.S. and son of second president John Adams, is born in Braintree, Massachusetts. Andrew Jackson, seventh president of the U.S., is born in Waxhaw settlement, South Carolina.

1769—Daniel Boone sights the Kentucky Territory.

1770—In the Boston Massacre, British soldiers kill five colonists and injure six. Townshend Acts are repealed, thus eliminating all duties on imports to the colonies except tea.

1771—Benjamin Franklin begins his autobiography, a work that he will never complete. The North Carolina assembly passes the "Bloody Act," which makes rioters guilty of treason.

1772—Samuel Adams rouses colonists to consider British threats to self-government. Thomas Jefferson marries Martha Wayles Skelton.

1773—English Parliament passes the Tea Act. Colonists dressed as Mohawk Indians board British tea ships and toss 342 casks of tea into the water in what becomes known as the Boston Tea Party. William Henry Harrison is born in Charles City County, Virginia.

1774—British close the port of Boston to punish the city for the Boston Tea Party. First Continental Congress convenes in Philadelphia.

1775—American Revolution begins with battles of Lexington and Concord, Massachusetts. Second Continental Congress opens in Philadelphia. George Washington becomes commander-in-chief of the Continental army.

1776—Declaration of Independence is adopted on July 4.

1777—Congress adopts the American flag with thirteen stars and thirteen stripes. John Adams is sent to France to negotiate peace treaty.

1778—France declares war against Great Britain and becomes U.S. ally.

1779—British surrender to Americans at Vincennes. Thomas Jefferson is elected governor of Virginia. James Madison is elected to the Continental Congress.

1780—Benedict Arnold, first American traitor, defects to the British.

1781—Articles of Confederation go into effect. Cornwallis surrenders to George Washington at Yorktown, ending the American Revolution.

1782—American commissioners, including John Adams, sign peace treaty with British in Paris. Thomas Jefferson's wife, Martha, dies. Martin Van Buren is born in Kinderhook, New York.

1784—Zachary Taylor is born near Barboursville, Virginia.

1785—Congress adopts the dollar as the unit of currency. John Adams is made minister to Great Britain. Thomas Jefferson is appointed minister to France.

1786—Shays' Rebellion begins in Massachusetts.

1787—Constitutional Convention assembles in Philadelphia, with George Washington presiding; U.S. Constitution is adopted. Delaware, New Jersey, and Pennsylvania become states.

1788—Virginia, South Carolina, New York, Connecticut, New Hampshire, Maryland, and Massachusetts become states. U.S. Constitution is ratified. New York City is declared U.S. capital.

1789—Presidential electors elect George Washington and John Adams as first president and vice-president. Thomas Jefferson is appointed secretary of state. North Carolina becomes a state. French Revolution begins.

1790—Supreme Court meets for the first time. Rhode Island becomes a state. First national census in the U.S. counts 3,929,214 persons. John Tyler is born in Charles City County, Virginia.

1791—Vermont enters the Union. U.S. Bill of Rights, the first ten amendments to the Constitution, goes into effect. District of Columbia is established.

1792—Thomas Paine publishes *The Rights of Man*. Kentucky becomes a state. Two political parties are formed in the U.S., Federalist and Republican. Washington is elected to a second term, with Adams as vice-president.

1793—War between France and Britain begins; U.S. declares neutrality. Eli Whitney invents the cotton gin; cotton production and slave labor increase in the South.

1794—Eleventh Amendment to the Constitution is passed, limiting federal courts' power. "Whiskey Rebellion" in Pennsylvania protests federal whiskey tax. James Madison marries Dolley Payne Todd.

1795—George Washington signs the Jay Treaty with Great Britain. Treaty of San Lorenzo, between U.S. and Spain, settles Florida boundary and gives U.S. right to navigate the Mississippi. James Polk is born near Pineville, North Carolina.

1796—Tennessee enters the Union. Washington gives his Farewell Address, refusing a third presidential term. John Adams is elected president and Thomas Jefferson vice-president.

1797—Adams recommends defense measures against possible war with France. Napoleon Bonaparte and his army march against Austrians in Italy. U.S. population is about 4,900,000.

1798—Washington is named commander-in-chief of the U.S. army. Department of the Navy is created. Alien and Sedition Acts are passed. Napoleon's troops invade Egypt and Switzerland.

1799—George Washington dies at Mount Vernon. James Monroe is elected governor of Virginia. French Revolution ends. Napoleon becomes ruler of France.

1800—Thomas Jefferson and Aaron Burr tie for president. U.S. capital is moved from Philadelphia to Washington, D.C. The White House is built as presidents' home. Spain returns Louisiana to France. Millard Fillmore is born in Locke, New York.

1801—After thirty-six ballots, House of Representatives elects Thomas Jefferson president, making Burr vice-president. James Madison is named secretary of state.

1802—Congress abolishes excise taxes. U.S. Military Academy is founded at West Point, New York.

1803—Ohio enters the Union. Louisiana Purchase treaty is signed with France, greatly expanding U.S. territory.

1804—Twelfth Amendment to the Constitution rules that president and vice-president be elected separately. Alexander Hamilton is killed by Vice-President Aaron Burr in a duel. Orleans Territory is established. Napoleon crowns himself emperor of France.

1805—Thomas Jefferson begins his second term as president. Lewis and Clark expedition reaches the Pacific Ocean.

1806—Coinage of silver dollars is stopped; resumes in 1836.

1807—Aaron Burr is acquitted in treason trial. Embargo Act closes U.S. ports to trade.

1808—James Madison is elected president. Congress outlaws importing slaves from Africa.

1810—U.S. population is 7,240,000.

1811—William Henry Harrison defeats Indians at Tippecanoe. Monroe is named secretary of state.

1812—Louisiana becomes a state. U.S. declares war on Britain (War of 1812). James Madison is reelected president. Napoleon invades Russia.

1813—British forces take Fort Niagara and Buffalo, New York.

1814—Francis Scott Key writes "The Star-Spangled Banner." British troops burn much of Washington, D.C., including the White House. Treaty of Ghent ends War of 1812. James Monroe becomes secretary of war.

1815—Napoleon meets his final defeat at Battle of Waterloo.

1816—James Monroe is elected president. Indiana becomes a state.

1817—Mississippi becomes a state. Construction on Erie Canal begins.

1818—Illinois enters the Union. The present thirteen-stripe flag is adopted. Border between U.S. and Canada is agreed upon.

1819—Alabama becomes a state. U.S. purchases Florida from Spain. Thomas Jefferson establishes the University of Virginia.

1820—James Monroe is reelected. In the Missouri Compromise, Maine enters the Union as a free (non-slave) state.

1821—Missouri enters the Union as a slave state. Santa Fe Trail opens the American Southwest. Mexico declares independence from Spain. Napoleon Bonaparte dies.

1822—U.S. recognizes Mexico and Colombia. Liberia in Africa is founded as a home for freed slaves.

1823—Monroe Doctrine closes North and South America to European colonizing or invasion.

1824—House of Representatives elects John Quincy Adams president when none of the four candidates wins a majority in national election. Mexico becomes a republic.

1825—Erie Canal is opened. U.S. population is 11,300,000.

1826—Thomas Jefferson and John Adams both die on July 4, the fiftieth anniversary of the Declaration of Independence.

1828—Andrew Jackson is elected president. Tariff of Abominations is passed, cutting imports.

1829—James Madison attends Virginia's constitutional convention. Slavery is abolished in Mexico.

1830—Indian Removal Act to resettle Indians west of the Mississippi is approved.

1831—James Monroe dies in New York City. James A. Garfield is born in Orange, Ohio. Cyrus McCormick develops his reaper.

1832—Andrew Jackson, nominated by the new Democratic Party, is reelected president.

1833—Britain abolishes slavery in its colonies.

1835—Federal government becomes debt-free for the first time.

1836—Martin Van Buren becomes president. Texas wins independence from Mexico. Arkansas joins the Union. James Madison dies at Montpelier, Virginia.

1837—Michigan enters the Union. U.S. population is 15,900,000.

1840—William Henry Harrison is elected president.

1841—President Harrison dies in Washington, D.C., one month after inauguration. Vice-President John Tyler succeeds him.

1844—James Knox Polk is elected president. Samuel Morse sends first telegraphic message.

1845—Texas and Florida become states. Potato famine in Ireland causes massive emigration from Ireland to U.S. Andrew Jackson dies near Nashville, Tennessee.

1846—Iowa enters the Union. War with Mexico begins.

1847—U.S. captures Mexico City.

1848—Zachary Taylor becomes president. Treaty of Guadalupe Hidalgo ends Mexico-U.S. war. Wisconsin becomes a state.

1849—James Polk dies in Nashville, Tennessee.

1850—President Taylor dies in Washington, D.C.; Vice-President Millard Fillmore succeeds him. California enters the Union, breaking tie between slave and free states.

1852—Franklin Pierce is elected president.

1853—Gadsden Purchase transfers Mexican territory to U.S.

1854—"War for Bleeding Kansas" is fought between slave and free states.

1855—Czar Nicholas I of Russia dies, succeeded by Alexander II.

1856—James Buchanan is elected president. In Massacre of Potawatomi Creek, Kansas-slavers are murdered by free-staters.

1858—Minnesota enters the Union. Theodore Roosevelt is born in New York City.

1859—Oregon becomes a state.

1860—Abraham Lincoln is elected president; South Carolina secedes from the Union in protest.

1861—Arkansas, Tennessee, North Carolina, and Virginia secede. Kansas enters the Union as a free state. Civil War begins.

1862—Union forces capture Fort Henry, Roanoke Island, Fort Donelson, Jacksonville, and New Orleans; Union armies are defeated at the battles of Bull Run and Fredericksburg. Martin Van Buren dies in Kinderhook, New York. John Tyler dies near Charles City, Virginia.

1863—Lincoln issues Emancipation Proclamation: all slaves held in rebelling territories are declared free. West Virginia becomes a state.

1864—Abraham Lincoln is reelected. Nevada becomes a state.

1865—Lincoln is assassinated, succeeded by Andrew Johnson. U.S. Civil War ends on May 26. Thirteenth Amendment abolishes slavery.

1867—Nebraska becomes a state. U.S. buys Alaska from Russia for $7,200,000. Reconstruction Acts are passed.

1868—President Johnson is impeached for violating Tenure of Office Act, but is acquitted by Senate. Ulysses S. Grant is elected president. Fourteenth Amendment prohibits voting discrimination.

1870—Fifteenth Amendment gives blacks the right to vote.

1872—Grant is reelected over Horace Greeley. General Amnesty Act pardons ex-Confederates.

1874—Millard Fillmore dies in Buffalo, New York. Herbert Hoover is born in West Branch, Iowa.

1876—Colorado enters the Union. "Custer's last stand": he and his men are massacred by Sioux Indians at Little Big Horn, Montana.

1877—Rutherford B. Hayes is elected president as all disputed votes are awarded to him.

1880—James A. Garfield is elected president.

1881—President Garfield is assassinated and dies in Elberon, New Jersey. Vice-President Chester A. Arthur succeeds him.

1882—U.S. bans Chinese immigration. Franklin D. Roosevelt is born in Hyde Park, New York.

1884—Harry S. Truman is born in Lamar, Missouri. Grover Cleveland becomes president.

1886—Statue of Liberty is dedicated.

1888—Benjamin Harrison is elected president.

1889—North Dakota, South Dakota, Washington, and Montana become states.

1890—Dwight D. Eisenhower is born in Denison, Texas. Idaho and Wyoming become states.

1892—Grover Cleveland is elected president.

1896—William McKinley is elected president. Utah becomes a state.

1898—U.S. declares war on Spain over Cuba.

1899—Philippines demand independence from U.S.

1900—McKinley is reelected. Boxer Rebellion against foreigners in China begins.

1901—McKinley is assassinated by anarchist; he is succeeded by Theodore Roosevelt.

1902—U.S. acquires perpetual control over Panama Canal.

1903—Alaskan frontier is settled.

1904—Russian-Japanese War breaks out. Theodore Roosevelt wins presidential election.

1905—Treaty of Portsmouth signed, ending Russian-Japanese War.

1906—U.S. troops occupy Cuba.

1907—President Roosevelt bars all Japanese immigration. Oklahoma enters the Union.

1908—William Howard Taft becomes president. Lyndon B. Johnson is born near Stonewall, Texas.

1909—NAACP is founded under W.E.B. DuBois

1910—China abolishes slavery.

1911—Chinese Revolution begins.

1912—Woodrow Wilson is elected president. Arizona and New Mexico become states.

1913—Federal income tax is introduced in U.S. through the Sixteenth Amendment. Richard Nixon is born in Yorba Linda, California.

1914—World War I begins.

1915—British liner *Lusitania* is sunk by German submarine.

1916—Wilson is reelected president.

1917—U.S. breaks diplomatic relations with Germany. Czar Nicholas of Russia abdicates as revolution begins. U.S. declares war on Austria-Hungary. John F. Kennedy is born in Brookline, Massachusetts.

1918—Wilson proclaims "Fourteen Points" as war aims. On November 11, armistice is signed between Allies and Germany.

1919—Eighteenth Amendment prohibits sale and manufacture of intoxicating liquors. Wilson presides over first League of Nations; wins Nobel Peace Prize. Theodore Roosevelt dies in Oyster Bay, New York.

1920—Nineteenth Amendment (women's suffrage) is passed. Warren Harding is elected president.

1921—Adolf Hitler's stormtroopers begin to terrorize political opponents.

1922—Irish Free State is established. Soviet states form USSR. Benito Mussolini forms Fascist government in Italy.

1923—President Harding dies; he is succeeded by Vice-President Calvin Coolidge.

1924—Coolidge is elected president.

1925—Hitler reorganizes Nazi Party and publishes first volume of *Mein Kampf.*

1926—Fascist youth organizations founded in Germany and Italy. Republic of Lebanon proclaimed.

1927—Stalin becomes Soviet dictator. Economic conference in Geneva attended by fifty-two nations.

1928—Herbert Hoover is elected president. U.S. and many other nations sign Kellogg-Briand pacts to outlaw war.

1929—Stock prices in New York crash on "Black Thursday"; the Great Depression begins.

1930—Bank of U.S. and its many branches close (most significant bank failure of the year).

1931—Emigration from U.S. exceeds immigration for first time as Depression deepens.

1932—Franklin D. Roosevelt wins presidential election in a Democratic landslide.

1933—First concentration camps are erected in Germany. U.S. recognizes USSR and resumes trade. Twenty-First Amendment repeals prohibition.

1934—Severe dust storms hit Plains states. President Roosevelt passes U.S. Social Security Act.

1936—Roosevelt is reelected. Spanish Civil War begins. Hitler and Mussolini form Rome-Berlin Axis.

1937—Roosevelt signs Neutrality Act.

1938—Roosevelt sends appeal to Hitler and Mussolini to settle European problems amicably.

1939—Germany takes over Czechoslovakia and invades Poland, starting World War II.

1940—Roosevelt is reelected for a third term.

1941—Japan bombs Pearl Harbor, U.S. declares war on Japan. Germany and Italy declare war on U.S.; U.S. then declares war on them.

1942—Allies agree not to make separate peace treaties with the enemies. U.S. government transfers more than 100,000 Nisei (Japanese-Americans) from west coast to inland concentration camps.

1943—Allied bombings of Germany begin.

1944—Roosevelt is reelected for a fourth term. Allied forces invade Normandy on D-Day.

1945—President Franklin D. Roosevelt dies in Warm Springs, Georgia; Vice-President Harry S. Truman succeeds him. Mussolini is killed; Hitler commits suicide. Germany surrenders. U.S. drops atomic bomb on Hiroshima; Japan surrenders: end of World War II.

1946—U.N. General Assembly holds its first session in London. Peace conference of twenty-one nations is held in Paris.

1947—Peace treaties are signed in Paris. "Cold War" is in full swing.

1948—U.S. passes Marshall Plan Act, providing $17 billion in aid for Europe. U.S. recognizes new nation of Israel. India and Pakistan become free of British rule. Truman is elected president.

1949—Republic of Eire is proclaimed in Dublin. Russia blocks land route access from Western Germany to Berlin; airlift begins. U.S., France, and Britain agree to merge their zones of occupation in West Germany. Apartheid program begins in South Africa.

1950—Riots in Johannesburg, South Africa, against apartheid. North Korea invades South Korea. U.N. forces land in South Korea and recapture Seoul.

1951—Twenty-Second Amendment limits president to two terms.

1952—Dwight D. Eisenhower resigns as supreme commander in Europe and is elected president.

1953—Stalin dies; struggle for power in Russia follows. Rosenbergs are executed for espionage.

1954—U.S. and Japan sign mutual defense agreement.

1955—Blacks in Montgomery, Alabama, boycott segregated bus lines.

1956—Eisenhower is reelected president. Soviet troops march into Hungary.

1957—U.S. agrees to withdraw ground forces from Japan. Russia launches first satellite, *Sputnik.*

1958—European Common Market comes into being. Alaska becomes the forty-ninth state. Fidel Castro begins war against Batista government in Cuba.

1959—Hawaii becomes fiftieth state. Castro becomes premier of Cuba. De Gaulle is proclaimed president of the Fifth Republic of France.

1960—Historic debates between Senator John F. Kennedy and Vice-President Richard Nixon are televised. Kennedy is elected president. Brezhnev becomes president of USSR.

1961—Berlin Wall is constructed. Kennedy and Khrushchev confer in Vienna. In Bay of Pigs incident, Cubans trained by CIA attempt to overthrow Castro.

1962—U.S. military council is established in South Vietnam.

1963—Riots and beatings by police and whites mark civil rights demonstrations in Birmingham, Alabama; 30,000 troops are called out, Martin Luther King, Jr., is arrested. Freedom marchers descend on Washington, D.C., to demonstrate. President Kennedy is assassinated in Dallas, Texas; Vice-President Lyndon B. Johnson is sworn in as president.

1964—U.S. aircraft bomb North Vietnam. Johnson is elected president. Herbert Hoover dies in New York City.

1965—U.S. combat troops arrive in South Vietnam.

1966—Thousands protest U.S. policy in Vietnam. National Guard quells race riots in Chicago.

1967—Six-Day War between Israel and Arab nations.

1968—Martin Luther King, Jr., is assassinated in Memphis, Tennessee. Senator Robert Kennedy is assassinated in Los Angeles. Riots and police brutality take place at Democratic National Convention in Chicago. Richard Nixon is elected president. Czechoslovakia is invaded by Soviet troops.

1969—Dwight D. Eisenhower dies in Washington, D.C. Hundreds of thousands of people in several U.S. cities demonstrate against Vietnam War.

1970—Four Vietnam War protesters are killed by National Guardsmen at Kent State University in Ohio.

1971—Twenty-Sixth Amendment allows eighteen-year-olds to vote.

1972—Nixon visits Communist China; is reelected president in near-record landslide. Watergate affair begins when five men are arrested in the Watergate hotel complex in Washington, D.C. Nixon announces resignations of aides Haldeman, Ehrlichman, and Dean and Attorney General Kleindienst as a result of Watergate-related charges. Harry S. Truman dies in Kansas City, Missouri.

1973—Vice-President Spiro Agnew resigns; Gerald Ford is named vice-president. Vietnam peace treaty is formally approved after nineteen months of negotiations. Lyndon B. Johnson dies in San Antonio, Texas.

1974—As a result of Watergate cover-up, impeachment is considered; Nixon resigns and Ford becomes president. Ford pardons Nixon and grants limited amnesty to Vietnam War draft evaders and military deserters.

1975—U.S. civilians are evacuated from Saigon, South Vietnam, as Communist forces complete takeover of South Vietnam.

1976—U.S. celebrates its Bicentennial. James Earl Carter becomes president.

1977—Carter pardons most Vietnam draft evaders, numbering some 10,000.

1980—Ronald Reagan is elected president.

1981—President Reagan is shot in the chest in assassination attempt. Sandra Day O'Connor is appointed first woman justice of the Supreme Court.

1983—U.S. troops invade island of Grenada.

1984—Reagan is reelected president. Democratic candidate Walter Mondale's running mate, Geraldine Ferraro, is the first woman selected for vice-president by a major U.S. political party.

1985—Soviet Communist Party secretary Konstantin Chernenko dies; Mikhail Gorbachev succeeds him. U.S. and Soviet officials discuss arms control in Geneva. Reagan and Gorbachev hold summit conference in Geneva. Racial tensions accelerate in South Africa.

1986—Space shuttle *Challenger* explodes shortly after takeoff; crew of seven dies. U.S. bombs bases in Libya. Corazon Aquino defeats Ferdinand Marcos in Philippine presidential election.

1987—Iraqi missile rips the U.S. frigate *Stark* in the Persian Gulf, killing thirty-seven American sailors. Congress holds hearings to investigate sale of U.S. arms to Iran to finance Nicaraguan *contra* movement.

Index
Page numbers in boldface type indicate illustrations.

About the Author

Dee Lillegard is the author of *September To September, Poems for All Year Round*, a teacher resource, and many easy readers, including titles for Childrens Press's *I Can Be* career series. For the *Encyclopedia of Presidents* series, she has written biographies of John Tyler, James K. Polk, James A. Garfield, and Richard Nixon. Over two hundred of Ms. Lillegard's stories, poems, and puzzles have appeared in numerous children's magazines. Ms. Lillegard lives in the San Francisco Bay Area, where she teaches Writing for Children.